Ace That Job Interview

Take Control and Sell Yourself
with Sincerity and Confidence

by Nordie Williams

Copyright 2015 Nordie Williams

All rights reserved. No part of this book may be reproduced in any form or by any means, electronic or otherwise, without the prior written consent of the author.

Acknowledgement:

Front cover image source: CreateSpace, reproduced with permission.

TABLE OF CONTENTS

Introduction	4
Preparing to Perform	5
First Impressions	7
Tell Me About Yourself	8
The Interactive Interview	11
The Behavioral Interview	12
What is Your Greatest Strength?	15
What is Your Greatest Weakness?	17
Why Did You Leave Your Previous Job?	21
Why Do You Want This Job?	22
Where Do You See Yourself Five Years From Now?	23
Why Should We Hire You?	24
What Are Your Salary Expectations?	25
Last Impressions and Exit Strategy	26
From the Interviewer's Perspective	27
Conclusion	29

INTRODUCTION

A job interview is normally conducted verbally and, contrary to writing your resume, you will not have a lot of time to consider your answers. To succeed, you must not only give the interviewer the types of answers he or she seeks, you must articulate them in a way that is likely to instill a positive impression of you and the belief that you are qualified for the job.

Most people are naturally nervous prior to and during an interview. The job you are interviewing for is important to you, and could potentially affect your financial future. An effective way to combat uncontrolled and destructive nervousness is by being rightly prepared. When you are rightly prepared, you will encounter few surprises and little will throw you off track.

Acing a job interview does not require plowing through hundreds of pages of suggestions on the subject, however. Nor does it require memorizing every conceivable question you might be asked, and every best answer. Although the interviewer may ask you any combination of questions drawn from a pool of hundreds of distinct subjects, your job of preparing for the interview will be a whole lot easier once you understand that most of these questions really ask about the same thing and lead back to the same objective: To determine whether or not you're a good fit.

The interviewer will disguise the questions in several ways; for instance, by asking about your greatest strengths and weaknesses, where you see yourself five years from now, or why they should hire you. This quick read will prepare you for the in-person job interview by giving you several specific pointers that you can use over and over by implementing minor modifications that give the interviewer the answers he or she seeks.

PREPARING TO PERFORM

Performing at the interview is important, because it might be your only chance of getting the job you want. Although it proves difficult to determine exactly what the interviewer is looking for, with a little bit of forethought, you can anticipate most questions you will be asked, and at the very least the most common ones, such as, Tell me about yourself; Why do you want to work for us; and, What are your salary expectations?

Some interviewers are looking for hard skills, such as technical expertise; others are looking for soft skills and personality traits, such as communication and leadership skills. Know in advance what your company is looking for so that you can prepare accordingly. How do you know? Start by reading the job description and requirements. If the job requires substantial customer contact or teamwork with others, or if it is a supervisor position, soft skills might be emphasized over hard skills. Such interviews are likely behavioral based. If the job is an engineering position, it might emphasize hard skills. But one set of job skills is not totally exclusive of the other. Engineering positions also require some form of soft skills, and customer service positions require a bit of hard skills. But it helps to know which ones will be prioritized in the interview. If you have had similar jobs in the past, it should lead you in the right direction.

Your road to this particular job might have been long. Rather than simply mentioning your schooling or past training and jobs, as you would in your resume, make an effort to indicate how past experiences have helped you grow into the position you are currently in or aspire to fill. The idea is to demonstrate that you didn't pick the job out of a hat, so to speak, but have a vested interest in the position.

Researching the job for which you are applying not only helps you answer tough interview questions, it demonstrates that you have done your homework and are serious enough about getting the job that you are willing to spend time learning about it. Researching and thinking about questions you might be asked also gives you confidence. Even if you don't remember every detail, it will make you feel rightly prepared and give the interviewer a positive perception of you. Having done your research can help you answer a wide variety of interview questions, such as, Why do you want to work here; How do you visualize using your skills to benefit our company; or, Why do you want to leave your current job? Answers to these questions and more can be drawn from research you have done about the company. The importance of doing your homework can therefore not be stressed enough.

It is normal to feel nervous about a job interview. It could after all have a significant impact on your economic future. One reason why we get nervous is because we feel that we are being evaluated and judged. This places the interviewer in the driver seat. As already stated, you can do a lot to alleviate nervousness by studying up on the company you are interviewing with and seriously thinking about commonly asked interview questions and how to answer them, but also by placing yourself in the driver seat and approaching the interview from the perspective that, although they are interviewing you, you are simultaneously interviewing them to determine if they are a good fit for your personality type and can give you a position that is rewarding to you both intellectually and financially. Ask, is this company professional and worthy enough to draw benefits from my expertise? How you approach the interview and how you come across to the interviewer, has much to do with your attitude about yourself and how you think they should view you.

FIRST IMPRESSIONS

It is our belief that first impressions are important; however, the reality is that a poor first impression is not necessarily indicative of poor work performance. Job interviews would be a whole lot easier if the interviewer looked deeper than beyond the first impression. Unfortunately, most job interviews are quite competitive. There may be hundreds or even thousands of applicants for a handful of jobs. So just how does the interviewer choose the right person for the job? It should be acknowledged that it is no easy task. By the end of the day, the interviewer will likely be tired, and the more tired he or she gets as the day wears on, the less likely he is to be attentive to factors outside of first impressions.

Dressing appropriately naturally goes without saying, so we're not going to say more about it. Just as appropriate dress is important in making a good first impression, so is posture. Stand up, smile, and offer your hand when the interviewer enters the room. Give a whole hand in the handshake, and a firm grip. Avoid shaking only the tip of the fingers. Not only does this type of handshake feel weak, some people find it offensive.

Pull your shoulders back and stand tall. Once asked to sit, don't get overly comfortable by sitting crouched or slouched to one side of your chair. Sitting upright or leaning forward slightly demonstrates alertness and interest. Make eye-contact and maintain eye-contact throughout the interview, also when you get a question that throws you off track momentarily. The interviewer will not merely remember how you answered the question, but also how you handled yourself when asked a difficult question.

TELL ME ABOUT YOURSELF

When asked to talk about yourself, the interviewer is likely less interested in hearing about your childhood or family, than about factors in your past that are relevant to the job. These include why you find the job attractive, and what expertise you believe you can bring to the company. Most answers should last no more than one to two minutes. Keeping your answers brief might prove particularly important when telling anecdotal stories about a prior occurrence, such as a situation where you used your communication skills successfully to solve a customer complaint.

How you used your past education and experiences is also more important and informative, than simply listing the schools you attended or the titles you hold. Stating that you have a master's degree in business administration is not as informative as explaining what you have done with that education and how you have utilized the skills you learned in graduate school. Although you may be entitled to attach PhD to the end of your name, if you can't demonstrate how you have used the skills you acquired in your studies, for the purpose of the job interview, the title itself is of little value.

Discussing your past, particularly what you have done and accomplished, also indicates where your ambitions lie, and is more important than discussing what you hope to accomplish at some future date. Don't say, "I have a master's degree in business with a 3.7 GPA. Although I haven't had the opportunity to use my degree yet, I hope to . . . " This statement demonstrates little about your ability to follow through or see an assignment to the end. Stating what you hope to do is just wishful thinking. Stating what you have done brings something concrete to the table.

Tell me about yourself, then, is an open-ended question. Open-ended questions give you opportunities to elaborate on your answer and make it lead somewhere of importance. When answered with forethought, it gives the interviewer useful information about you. The "tell me about yourself" question is therefore a great opportunity to lead the interviewer back to the job you are seeking, and to tie your prior education and work experiences to the new position. A good answer should tell the interviewer what is important to you. Your loyalties should lie with the job for which you are applying, and not with your family or hobbies.

So where do you start? Start by talking about your previous work related experiences, why you excelled, and why you are a good match for this particular company. Talk briefly about your strengths. If you want to include something personal, rather than telling them how many children you have, find something unique (after all, having kids is not unique), such as work experience in a foreign firm or country, or foreign language studies and how these might help you in the position for which you are applying.

Once focus is placed on what you have done, you can turn briefly to what you wish to accomplish in your new position. This is a good opportunity for mentioning continuing education, such as evening classes or online courses, rather than traditional education, such as college and graduate school, which should be included in your resume, anyway. Mentioning continuing education demonstrates that you understand that life and work are learning processes, and that learning doesn't end with your college degree. It demonstrates that you have a hunger for knowledge and are willing to spend time and effort acquiring it. This, in turn, demonstrates ambition, which looks a whole lot better than stating that you want this job simply because you need some way of paying your bills and feeding your family.

THE INTERACTIVE INTERVIEW

Now, then, that you have made your first impression and told them briefly about yourself, what type of interview might you expect and how should you act?

A job interview is meant to be interactive. Although the impression is probably that the interviewer is in charge, nothing says that you have to view it this way. Seize the initiative every time an opportunity presents itself, which is pretty much every time they ask a question. This places you in the driver seat and allows you to guide the interview to your advantage. Seizing the initiative is not about interrupting the interviewer or rambling senselessly for long periods of time, but about having a list of good answers prepared, having done your homework about the company, and being ready to discuss your qualifications. When seizing the initiative, you also demonstrate confidence, competence, and comfort with the idea of working at this particular company.

Most job interviews will be built on a series of open-ended questions and, as already discussed, answering open-ended questions naturally requires some elaboration. Interacting with the interviewer requires more than answering with a simple yes or no. If the interviewer looks at your resume and says, "I can see here that you have good communication skills," don't affirm the statement with a simple "yes." Add something that demonstrates why this is true. The same goes for hard skills. If the interviewer says he can see from your resume that you designed product X, then talk a bit about the skills that were involved in this accomplishment.

Interaction can also take the form of counter-questions about the position sought. When you build on the interviewer's questions by asking counter-questions, you will likely uncover detailed information that will prove helpful in guiding you toward better answers for the remainder of the interview. If you're applying for a technical position, for instance, asking technical questions that pertain to a particular problem you are likely to encounter in your job, demonstrates that you have prior knowledge of the type of environment you will be working in and that you are comfortable with it. Asking counter-questions also demonstrates that you are hungry for information about the job and the company. People who ask questions are looking for ways to improve themselves, and this is usually a good character trait to have.

THE BEHAVIORAL INTERVIEW

Depending on the type of job you are interviewing for, then, and in order to determine if you will be a good fit, the interviewer will likely be interested in your personality traits. If they are hiring for a leadership position, you must naturally work well with others, and they might be looking for someone who can lead without appearing abrasive. They might also be looking for someone who is well-organized and has vision, and who is ready to deal proactively and objectively with behavioral problems within the workforce. How do they know if you possess these character traits? One way is by asking about your past and how you handled a particular situation.

The behavioral interview asks you about past behaviors in order to predict future performance. It might help the interviewer determine why one candidate is more likely to succeed with this company than another. It includes questions that generally start with, Tell me about a time when . . .; How did you handle . . .; or, Name a situation that . . .

You can naturally not anticipate all types of behavioral based questions you might be asked, but you can certainly anticipate and prepare to answer some of the more common ones. Preparing an answer in advance of the interview will give you confidence to answer the question. Some of the questions can be anticipated by looking at the required qualifications for the position. If the job requirements include great communication skills, critical thinking skills, or problem solving and teamwork skills, then consider in advance of the interview a brief story that takes about a minute to tell, and that describes how you used these sorts of skills in the past. For example, if the job involves sales or contract negotiations, you might mention that a good negotiation skill when closing a deal is to ensure that all parties feel satisfied. Tell a brief story of how you achieve this. In a sales position, if you agree to more concessions than you should have, you will likely not feel satisfied. And if the customer didn't get a good value for the price, they will not feel satisfied, either.

If the job involves plenty of customer contact, you may be asked how you would deal with a situation involving a dissatisfied customer. By learning about how you have handled similar situations in the past, the interviewer can make an easier determination as to the likelihood that you can handle a future situation involving similar difficulties.

If asked if you prefer working with others or working alone, the best answer may depend on the situation and timing. If the job requires teamwork, then find a way to indicate why you like working with others while still communicating that you can also work alone. For example, you might emphasize how a well-honed team can get a lot done and do it well, and you enjoy participating in this well-oiled machined. But sometimes your unique skills also require that you tackle a specific problem alone, while finding ways for others to best utilize their unique skills. For instance, you might say that you are a disciplined self-starter, but realize that you couldn't get beyond the starting point and reach near the success you have, without the ability to draw information from the resources of your coworkers.

If the job requires working alone, then emphasize your strengths without necessarily saying that you prefer working alone. For example, you might bring to light that while you have the endurance required to tackle a tough problem and reach a solution, you also realize that others have unique skills, too, and you are willing to seek their help when necessary. Both teamwork and individual work requires certain skills. Working with others requires cooperation; working alone requires analytical skills. But they also overlap to some degree, and you want to emphasize this overlap, so that you come across as individually strong, yet cooperative.

It is also a good idea to bring a notepad to the interview, with brief remarks that will jog your memory for different situations you might be asked to elaborate on. Bringing a notepad with notes gives the impression that you are not only enthusiastic about the job, but also well-prepared.

WHAT IS YOUR GREATEST STRENGTH?

When asked about your greatest strength, use concrete examples that the interviewer can relate to. Instead of saying that you have great communication skills, mention what types of communication you do and what you have accomplished by communicating well. How can you use your excellent communication skills to benefit this particular company in the particular position for which you are applying?

Are you creative and imaginative? Well, don't stop there, because it tells the interviewer little about you. Give an example of how you have used your creativity and imagination, and the positive results it brought. Demonstrate through a concrete example how your background and knowledge will prove helpful for future tasks. Giving concrete examples is more important than merely talking about what type of work you enjoy doing. Rather than saying that you enjoy helping customers, name a specific example of how you used your customer service skills to help others, and how it created a win-win for both the customer and company.

Your strengths, then, whether hard or soft, should not be listed in simple one or two-word sentences. You must interpret them for the interviewer in order to demonstrate how the company will benefit. When you talk about your strengths, the examples you give should demonstrate in what ways they are unique and why the company should hire you. The interviewer is not looking to hire the average person, but somebody who can bring something unique to the table. Stating that you are a hard worker, that you come to work on time, or that you communicate well with others, sounds much too average and doesn't really bring anything unique to the table. Hard worker, how? Being on time, well, that's expected of you anyway. Communicate well with others, how? It is possible to talk about your strengths without making it sound as though you are sitting on your high horse. You are not telling the interviewer that you are better than him or her, but rather how and why you are a good match. Are you a responsible person? Then how? Give an example. Are you a self-starter? Then how? Give an example.

Likewise, if asked about your best accomplishment rather than your greatest strength, preferably tell them about something job related. If that is not possible, at the very least find a way to tie your best accomplishment to the job. For example, completing graduate school may in your view be your greatest accomplishment. You must now relate it to your job performance. How did graduate school help you perform better on the job? Give a specific example. Completing graduate school can also demonstrate that you have tenacity and ability to finish what you start.

When talking about your strengths, make an effort to sound sincere and demonstrate that you really believe in what you're saying. Sincerity comes easy when you are prepared to give real-life examples.

WHAT IS YOUR GREATEST WEAKNESS?

Interviewers will also commonly ask you to name at least one weakness. You may be able to identify your strengths, such as good communication skills, good problem solving skills, ability to perform well on teams, etc., but talking about your weaknesses might prove tougher. Talking about our weaknesses is uncomfortable, not only because we are reluctant to admit to having weaknesses (after all, if we portray our weaknesses, the interviewer might not want to hire us), but because we often don't take time to identify and assess our weaknesses.

First, you want to portray strength and not weakness in the most important job qualifications; that is, those that are listed as required for the job. If the job description says you need good communication skills, or good problem solving skills, make sure you discuss these as your strong points by giving specific examples, and choose something else as your weakness, something that is not listed, or at least not highly prioritized on the list of qualifications. If the job requires a lot of independent work, name one of your weaknesses as not very good at teamwork. If it requires teamwork, say that you need to improve your skills at working independently.

Second, remember that a weakness is only a weakness if you don't know how to prevent it from interfering with your performance. You need to find a way to turn your weaknesses into strengths. For instance, rather than saying that you are overly critical of others, which tends to cause friction between you and those with whom you interact, you might say that knowing that you are somewhat of a perfectionist, you make a special effort every day to compliment others on something they did especially well. Expect to be asked about your weaknesses and make sure you have an answer prepared before going to the interview, and that your answer highlights how you deal with your weaknesses.

Third, consider what personality traits make you a good candidate for the job. Many such traits can be stated either in the positive or negative, even though their basic characteristics haven't changed. For example, if you sense that the interviewer is looking for someone who is assertive and strong, then say that you are assertive and strong, and give an example. But if you have to work with a large group of people and this assertiveness causes disharmony within the work group and interferes with their ability to do their job to their fullest potential, say instead that you are a person of action with the ability to draw useful information from other people's experiences.

Thus, when you reveal your weakness, recognize that it can also be a strength depending on how you use it or how it is timed to the surrounding circumstances. Being a perfectionist is a weakness only if it causes disharmony among others, or if it decreases performance. But it is a strength if you use it correctly, because it minimizes errors and increases customer satisfaction. Having an outgoing personality is a weakness only if you run your mouth to the point that it interferes with or frustrates others trying to do their job. But it is a strength if you time it correctly, for example, by welcoming new members to the workforce and demonstrating a genuine interest in their successes and trials.

Fourth, demonstrate where you used to be and where you are now; in other words, what you have done to overcome your weakness. For instance, you might say that you used to be self-absorbed, which made you appear unfriendly to your coworkers. But you have largely overcome that by reminding yourself every day when coming to work to make eye-contact and smile at the first person you meet. If your greatest weakness is that you are unable to hold your horses, or that you overreact when angry, what are you doing to overcome it? For instance, you might say that every time something happens that contributes to a negative reaction, you have resolved to take a five-minute time-out to think about the best way to handle it. Contrary to our fears, having a weakness is not a deterrent to getting the job, but you must demonstrate some way in which you compensate for it.

Thus, when talking about your weaknesses, it helps if you can give a brief example of when you used a weakness to reach a positive outcome, and the results of doing so. A common interview question is, "Tell me about a time when . . ." Try to relate your answer to one of your weaknesses, and demonstrate how you handled the situation for the best possible outcome. When you explain why you behave a certain way, such as why you are a perfectionist or why you have a tendency to overreact if others don't meet your standards, it can appear as a strength and reflect not only self-awareness but confidence. When you are aware of having behaved inappropriately, mention what you learned from the experience and how you changed your future behavior.

Let's look at another example. Let's say, for instance, that your type-A personality involves some good qualities, such as always finishing assignments on time or early. But on occasion it also causes friction among others in a teamwork setting, because you often feel you could get the job done quicker and better alone. Since much work involves teamwork, you realize that you must be respectful of other people's feelings and give them a fair chance to complete their tasks. To make others feel appreciated, you are therefore making a special effort always to compliment them on work they did well. Instead of trying to overcome your weaknesses, say that you believe it is better to focus on building your strengths and, if possible, delegate assignments where you know you are weak to others who are strong in those areas. Emphasize that a good team is strong because its members have complementary skills, and not because they have similar or identical skills. But knowing what those complementary skills are requires knowing something about others, which also requires taking an interest in your coworkers or subordinates.

You might add that you recognize how diversity brings strength to the workplace, and that those who are less organized often have other qualities that, if utilized properly, will make the company overall stronger. Mention that the trick is placing others in positions that allow them to shine.

That said, when asking about your greatest weakness, the interviewer may not really care about your answer, or even how you overcame your weakness, but may be more concerned with how aware you are of your personality traits. Self-awareness can prove important, for example, in a position that requires leadership skills or a lot of interaction with other employees or customers.

Lastly, when asked about your greatest weakness, realize that whether it is a weakness or a strength is a matter of timing. Whether an outgoing personality is a weakness or strength is a matter of timing. The same goes for attention to detail or perfectionism. Are you bossy or assertive? Whether a particular trait is a weakness or a strength depends on how the group perceives you, and how they perceive you is often a matter of timing, or as has been said: It's the tone that makes the music. Once you understand this, you can turn any weakness into a strength.

WHY DID YOU LEAVE YOUR PREVIOUS JOB?

You will likely be asked why you left your previous job, or why you are planning on leaving. If the truth is that you hated your boss and didn't get along with your coworkers, speaking the truth bluntly will do you no favors. Nor will saying that you took that job just because you needed something to hold you over until you could find something better. These sorts of answers will make you come across as abrasive and not very dependable, and the interviewer will be reluctant to hire you, particularly if your new job requires substantial interaction with others. It is better to say that you're looking for new challenges or better opportunities for growth, and that you believe this company would be a good match for your ambitions.

WHY DO YOU WANT THIS JOB?

The reality might be that you want this job simply because you are unemployed. But if this is the case, it helps if you have a somewhat more informative answer ready, because you might have to explain your unemployment. For instance, you might be unemployed because your spouse had to relocate to another state with his or her company, which means that you voluntarily left your last job. But now that you have settled into your new home, you wish to enter the workforce again and make good use of your skills. Avoid a simple answer, such as how you have fallen on bad economic times and need to boost your income with a second job.

Thus, when asked why you want this particular job, your answer should demonstrate something positive and powerful about you, such as the fact that you welcome the challenges listed in the job description, and you see it as an opportunity to grow with the company. Focus on how you will be an asset to the company. You might mention something brief about their history, their age, or how they started and what they focus on. Include some detail that impressed you or that makes you particularly keen on working for this company.

Most jobs get boring with time, and many jobs become the same mundane grind every day. But you might still get asked about your motivations. The way to combat boredom, any kind of boredom, is through meaningful activity. But saying that you want a challenging position that involves problem solving and critical thinking doesn't really tell them much. Name some of the job requirements and why you would find them challenging and meaningful. Be specific and state exactly what types of challenges you are looking for, or better, what you have excelled at in the past.

WHERE DO YOU SEE YOURSELF FIVE YEARS FROM NOW?

When asking this question, the interviewer is probably looking for an indication that you have thought about your future and aspirations, because this tells him several things about you. For instance, it indicates whether or not you will be a good match, what your ambitions are, and if you are planning to stick around for awhile. If you demonstrate ambition and vision, you will also demonstrate that you are committed to doing a good job for this company.

Like most questions in the job interview, the question of where you see yourself in five years must be answered based on knowledge about the company and yourself. You must therefore study the company's history and aspirations before going to the interview. The specific answer may not be as important as the fact that you have a plan or an idea of what you wish to achieve, however. Not caring about your future enough to have dreams and aspirations, reflects poorly on you as a candidate for the job.

Talking about where you want to be in the future also gives the interviewer an indication of whether you are planning a career with this company, or if you just want this job to hold you over until something better comes along. If the latter is the case, not only will they likely not hire you, they will feel reluctant to invest in your education, training, and eventual promotion. Naturally, your answer should relate to the job. Don't tell them what type of house you see yourself living in five years from now.

WHY SHOULD WE HIRE YOU?

In contrast to the question why you want this job, which focuses on you, the question why they should hire you, focuses on them. It is important to understand that no company will hire you if they don't believe that your skills will increase their value. To answer why they should hire you, you must know why they are seeking to hire additional personnel at this time. Make sure you know what types of skills are required for the job, and that you can talk about those skills and competencies.

As in the question why you want this job, they might well ask you why you want to work for them in particular, and what you hope to achieve that would not be possible by working for the competition. This, too, requires doing some research about the company's goals and how they coincide with your personal goals. If you do your research properly, you might also be able to mention something about the competition and how they differ.

So why should they hire you? The obvious answer is that they should hire you because you have the qualities they are seeking in a job applicant. You know what those qualities are by doing your homework and reading the job description. In addition, you should state the unique qualities that you can bring to the table. Offer them something that sets you apart from others, or at least appears to set you apart.

Tell them about some unique training or insights that you have acquired. And, of course, indicate how you're in tune with the company's vision and values, and that you are enthusiastic about the job.

It's possible that you will be asked some off-road questions, such as what in particular makes you unique and what skills you have that nobody else has. Recognize that this question really leads back to your greatest strength, which is what makes you better suited for this job than anyone else. They're not looking for a jack-of-all-trades answer here, or someone who is good at everything (everyone is good at something, and if you list all of your skills, someone else will likely have at least some of these skills, too), but rather one unique skill that sets you apart.

WHAT ARE YOUR SALARY EXPECTATIONS?

One of the tougher questions to answer might be how much you expect to get paid. This may or may not be asked, depending on what type of position you are applying for. But if it is, then, again, be specific and prepared to support your answer with a reason for your request, such as your long and successful background.

If you are asked how much you expect to get paid, you are probably applying for a merit position of some sort, so it would be inappropriate to answer that you would be happy getting whatever everyone else is getting. It would also be inappropriate to underrate yourself, and say that you are willing to start at a lower scale and work your way up. You should have researched the position and have some idea of what it pays, and then ask for a specific figure and take it from there. When you state a specific figure that is not too low, you also demonstrate that you have confidence in your abilities, have done your research, and are therefore worthy of that figure. You want to remain within reasonable boundaries, of course, and not ask for twice the customary pay. Your salary has to be proper and based on your experience.

For instance, you might say, "Based on my research and knowledge of this position, I expect . . ." If possible, throw in something about your experience. For example, state that based on your long experience, you would expect to get paid in the upper level of the salary range for this position. You might also ask a counter-question about what salary range they are considering paying you.

LAST IMPRESSIONS AND EXIT STRATEGY

Just as first impressions are important, so are last impressions. These are often what the interviewer will remember you by. You must therefore have an appropriate exit strategy. In short, you want to remind the interviewer of the skills you can bring to the company and why they should hire you. Following up a day or two after the interview with a brief thank-you note will keep you on their mind and may trigger a positive decision almost instantly.

At the close of the interview, they will likely ask if you have any questions. Make sure to have some prepared. Saying, no thanks, you don't have any questions at the moment, demonstrates lack of enthusiasm or interest. Ask at least one or two pertinent questions that would not seem offensive (don't ask about a pay raise, or when you can take your first vacation). A good question might be about opportunities to improve on your current skills, such as training opportunities within the company. This demonstrates that your goal is to stay with this company for a long time, and that you are concerned with improving on current skills so that you can become the best possible asset for them.

You can also ask about something you have come across during your research of the company. Most people like to talk about themselves, particularly when somebody demonstrates interest. This includes the interviewer. If you ask something about the company, the interviewer will likely love to tell you about it.

A good way to exit after you have asked any questions you may have, is to ask what you can expect next and when you might hear from them regarding the results of the interview and position. This demonstrates that your mind is set on getting the job; you expect a job offer and are interested enough to be anxious to know the next step. Ask when you can expect to start if hired, what type of initial training to expect, and what the first few weeks will be like.

FROM THE INTERVIEWER'S PERSPECTIVE

When leaving the interview, how do you read the interviewer? How should you feel about what just transpired? If the interviewer took detailed notes, he or she was probably interested in your answers and how they related to the job requirements. If they did not take detailed notes or did not take notes at all, they were probably more interested in how you carried yourself or how quickly you responded to tough questions. They were probably more interested in your personality traits than in your specific answers. Lack of detailed note taking, however, might complicate the interviewer's ability to make a constructive comparison of job candidates they have interviewed. They might already have made up their mind about who they want to hire and are just going through the paces, so that it looks as though they are giving everybody a fair chance. This might be more common when interviewing for positions within a company for which you are already working.

Some job candidates answer interview questions with short phrases or single words; others like to talk at length about themselves and are keen on asking counter-questions. Both approaches tell the interviewer volumes about the personality traits of the candidate. But interviewers, too, can jump on the bandwagon and ask the same traditional irrelevant questions that have been asked for ages, without really knowing how these questions or answers contribute to their decision to hire or not hire a candidate. What is your greatest weakness? The answer to this question could prove important if the position for which you are applying is particularly sensitive to how you might overcome specific problems. But in many jobs, it is not important to overall performance whether or not you are aware of your greatest weakness, or are striving to overcome it.

Some questions are asked just because, which is an indication of weak interviewing skills. Stories of how a handful of candidates overcame their particular weaknesses may not make the interviewer any wiser about who is better suited for the job. What you answer may sometimes prove completely irrelevant. In the end, it might simply boil down to whether or not the interviewer liked you and was able to establish the right kind of rapport. Thus, chance, timing, and the people skills of both the interviewer and job candidate play a role.

CONCLUSION

To sum up, and assuming that the interviewer is skilled and attentive to your answers, most questions you can expect to be asked lead back to a single objective: To determine whether or not you will be a good fit. The best way to prepare for the interview is therefore to do enough research about the company to have at least some basic knowledge of their history and vision. Regardless of which questions you are asked, a wealth of information can be drawn from this background knowledge and related to your answers regarding your strengths and weaknesses, why you want the job, and how you can contribute to the future success of the company. Taking to heart the suggestions in this brief book should help you prepare for and get through a tough interview with confidence.

www.ingramcontent.com/pod-product-compliance
Lightning Source LLC
Chambersburg PA
CBHW070733180526
45167CB00004B/1730

* 9 7 8 1 5 0 6 0 3 3 3 6 5 *